t

wi, D0276558

in our Lord,

Fiona & Les

24.07.11

DAILY
Pathways

THE HELEN STEINER RICE FOUNDATION

Whatever the celebration, whatever the day, whatever the event, whatever the occasion, Helen Steiner Rice possessed the ability to express the appropriate feeling for that particular moment in time.

A happening became happier, a sentiment more sentimental, a memory more memorable because of her deep sensitivity to put into understandable language the emotion being experienced. Her positive attitude, her concern for others, and her love of God are identifiable threads woven into her life, her works . . . and even her death.

Prior to her passing, she established the HELEN STEINER RICE FOUNDATION, a nonprofit corporation whose purpose is to award grants to worthy charitable programs that aid the elderly, the needy, and the poor. In her lifetime, these were the individuals about whom Mrs. Rice was greatly concerned.

Royalties from the sale of this book will add to the financial capabilities of the HELEN STEINER RICE FOUNDATION, thus making possible additional grants. Each year this foundation presents grants, ranging from three thousand to fifteen thousand dollars each, to various, qualified, worthwhile, and charitable programs. Because of her foresight, her caring, and her deep convictions, Helen Steiner Rice continues to touch a countless number of lives. Thank you for your assistance in helping to keep Helen's dream alive.

Virginia J. Ruehlmann, Administrator

The Helen Steiner Rice Foundation

Suite 2100, Atrium Two

221 E. Fourth Street

Cincinnati, Ohio 45201

DAILY

Pathways

Helen Steiner Rice

Prayers by Virginia J. Ruehlmann

HUTCHINSON
London Sydney Auckland Johannesburg

Illustrations by Susanne DeMarco

© 1989 by Virginia Ruehlmann and
The Helen Steiner Rice Foundation

The rights of Helen Steiner Rice to be identified as Author of this work has been asserted by Helen Steiner Rice in accordance with the Copyright, Design and Patent Act, 1988

This edition first published in 1990 by Hutchinson
Reprinted 1991
Reprinted 1994

Random Century Group Ltd
20 Vauxhall Bridge Road, London SW1V 2SA
Random Century Australia (Pty) Ltd
20 Alfred Street, Milsons Point, Sydney, NSW 2061, Australia

Random Century New Zealand Ltd
PO Box 40–086, Glenfield, Auckland 10, New Zealand

Random Century South Africa (Pty) Ltd
PO Box 337, Bergvlei, 2012, South Africa

British Library Cataloguing in Publication Data

Rice, Helen Steiner
Daily pathways.
I. Title
811.54

ISBN 0-09-174586-1

Printed in Singapore by Tien Wah Press (Pte) Ltd.

To my husband,
who travels life's pathways
with
Christlike behavior,
concern for others,
love for his family,
and devotion to his Creator

Contents

You will show me the path to life,
  fullness of joys in your presence,
  the delights at your right hand forever.
                              Psalm 16:11 NAB

In his lifetime each individual has the opportunity to travel many diverse pathways. The direction that is chosen or the particular pathway selected is often determined by personal knowledge or perspective or intuitive sense.

As do all human beings, Helen Steiner Rice had many pathways from which to pick. Always her direction was determined by her trust in her Creator. Her childlike faith and implicit trust in God guided, sustained, and enabled her to travel, allegorically speaking, "rocky roads, smooth surfaced streets, garden walks, or mountainous trails." She appropriately put into understandable language the thoughts, the beliefs, the inspirations which she experienced during these journeys with God as her Guide.

This collection of significant passages of Scripture, profoundly meaningful poems by Mrs. Rice, and selections of personal prayers, praise, and petitions has been planned and mapped to assist you on your journey to inner peace.

As you read *Daily Pathways* may the message, meditation, and meaning support and direct you as you progress on your own pathway of life.

May you arrive safely at your destination!

                              Virginia J. Ruehlmann

Pathways

Memory builds a little pathway
That goes winding through my heart.
It's a lovely, quiet, gentle trail
From other things apart;
I only meet when traveling there
The folks I like the best
For this road I call remembrance
Is hidden from the rest;
But I hope I'll always find you
In my memory rendezvous
For I keep this little secret place
To meet with folks like you.

Hope

May God, the source of all patience and encouragement, enable you to live in perfect harmony with one another according to the spirit of Christ Jesus, so that with one heart and voice you may glorify God, the Father of our Lord Jesus Christ.

Romans 15:5, 6 NAB

Sometimes we feel uncertain
And unsure of everything.
Afraid to make decisions,
Dreading what the day will bring.

God has given us the answers
Which too often go unheeded,
But if we search His promises
We'll find everything that's needed.

So cast your burden on Him,
Seek His counsel when distressed,
And go to Him for comfort
When you're lonely and oppressed.
For God is our encouragement
In trouble and in trials,
And in suffering and in sorrow
He will turn our tears to smiles.

Encourage me, Father, as I strive to overcome these pangs of loneliness. Show me that a frown is really a smile turned upside down and then soothe me and help to alter my expression.

Worry can rob you of happiness, but kind words will cheer you up.

Proverbs 12:25 TEV

Happiness is something that is never far away,
It's as close as the things we do and we say—
So start out today with a smile on your face
And make this old world a happier place.

Support me, Lord, so that I know when to speak to encourage someone and when to remain silent.

O God, from my youth thou hast taught me, and I still proclaim thy wondrous deeds. So even to old age and gray hairs, O God, do not forsake me, till I proclaim thy might to all the generations to come.

Psalm 71:17, 18

Why am I cast down
    and despondently sad
When I long to be happy
    and joyous and glad?
And then with God's help
    it all becomes clear,
The soul has its seasons
    just the same as the year—
I too must pass through
    life's autumn of dying,
A desolate period
    of heart-hurt and crying,
Bounteous seasons
    and barren ones, too,
Times for rejoicing
    and times to be blue,
But I'm content in the knowledge
    that autumn-time sadness
Will surely be followed
    by a springtime of gladness.

Father, Your plan calls for the year to have seasons, and so too my life. Help me to enjoy the gifts, the blessings, the modifications that come with each year of my life.

And do not seek what you are to eat and what you are to drink, nor be of anxious mind. For all the nations of the world seek these things; and your Father knows that you need them. Instead, seek his kingdom, and these things shall be yours as well.

Luke 12:29–31

If friends disappoint you
 and plans go astray
And nothing works out
 in just the right way,
And you feel you have failed
 in achieving your goal,
And that life wrongly placed you
 in an unfitting role . . .
Take heart and stand tall
 and think who you are,
For God is your Father
 and no one can bar
Or keep you from reaching
 your desired success,
Or withhold the joy
 that is yours to possess . . .
But seek first His Kingdom
 and you will possess
The world's greatest riches
 which is true happiness.

Lord, if I have wisdom, I also have You. If You are with me and I continue to seek Your Kingdom, my wisdom has served me well, for true happiness will be mine.

So whatever you wish that men would do to you, do
so to them; for this is the law and the prophets.

Matthew 7:12

You'll find when you smile
your day will be brighter
And all of your burdens will seem
so much lighter.
For each time you smile you will find it is true
Somebody, somewhere will smile back at you,
And nothing on earth
can make life more worthwhile
Than the sunshine and warmth
of a beautiful smile.

*Dear God, I feel so generous. I want to give a smile away
each and every day that I live. Especially, I want to share
the smiles with those folk who don't seem to have any of
their own. Smiling is a study in arithmetic: By dividing one
smile between two persons, you subtract tension and add
some joy. Usually the original smile has been multiplied.*

O Lord, my God, I call for help by day; I cry out in the night before thee. Let my prayer come before thee, incline thy ear to my cry! For my soul is full of troubles. . . .

Psalm 88:1–3

I'm looking out the window
      and the day is drab and dreary,
And I'm trying to console myself
      by thinking something cheery
I know it's simply horrible
      to get in such a slump
And I also know it's up to me
      to get across this hump.
But I know that all the dark days
      are just part of God's plan;
We should accept them graciously
      and do the best we can . . .
So I'll just keep on trying
      for I know it's "Gospel true"
There never was a cloud so dark
      the sun could not shine through!

Mender of broken dreams, are You aware of the tears that I shed? Father, I know that You love and care about each bird and each lily in the field. Please do the same for me. Love me and care for me.

Joy and Peace

May the God of hope fill you with all joy and peace in believing, so that by the power of the Holy Spirit you may abound in hope.

Romans 15:13

God gives us a power we so seldom employ
For we're so unaware it is filled with such joy.
And the gift that God gives us is anticipation
Which we can fulfill with sincere expectation
For there's power in belief when we think we
    will find
Joy for the heart and sweet peace for the mind.
Just believing the day will bring a surprise
Is not only pleasant but surprisingly wise.
For we open the door to let joy walk through
When we learn to expect the best and most too
And believing we'll find a happy surprise
Makes reality out of a fancied surmise!

Today is a gift from You, God. Permit me to use it to the fullest, for by midnight tonight it will be gone forever.

Good is the LORD to one who waits for him,
    to the soul that seeks him;
It is good to hope in silence
    for the saving help of the LORD.
                        Lamentations 3:25, 26 NAB

Silently the green leaves grow
In silence falls the soft, white snow
Silently the flowers bloom
In silence sunshine fills a room
Silently bright stars appear
In silence velvet night draws near . . .
And silently God enters in
To free a troubled heart from sin
For God works silently in lives
For nothing spiritual survives
Amid the din of a noisy street
Where raucous crowds with hurrying feet
And "blinded eyes" and "deafened ear"
Are never privileged to hear
The message God wants to impart
To every troubled, weary heart
For only in a quiet place
Can man behold God face-to-face!

*Improve my senses, Lord, so that I can appreciate the
wonders of Your creation.*

See what love the Father has bestowed on us in letting us be called children of God! Yet that is what we are. The reason the world does not recognize us is that it never recognized the Son. Dearly beloved, we are God's children now; what we shall later be has not yet come to light. We know that when it comes to light we shall be like him, for we shall see him as he is.

1 John 3:1, 2 NAB

The silent stars in timeless skies
The wonderment in children's eyes,
The autumn haze, the breath of spring,
The chirping song the crickets sing,
A rosebud in a slender vase
Are all reflections of God's face.

God, if I just have the ability to see and the wisdom to comprehend, I can find You everywhere.

19

Ever since God created the world, his invisible qualities, both his eternal power and his divine nature, have been clearly seen; they are perceived in the things that God has made. . . .

Romans 1:20 TEV

> "The earth is the Lord's
>   and the fulness thereof"—
> It speaks of His greatness,
>   it sings of His love,
> I watch the night vanish
>   as a new day is born,
> And I hear the birds sing
>   on the wings of the morn,
> I see the dew glisten
>   in crystal-like splendor
> While God, with a touch
>   that is gentle and tender,
> Wraps up the night
>   and tucks it away
> And hangs out the sun
>   to herald a new day,
> A day yet unblemished
>   by what's gone before,
> A chance to begin
>   and start over once more.

Creator God, deepen my awareness of all that You have done to bring this world into existence and permit me to take time to enjoy Your gifts and Your awesome creations.

Artist of Artists

For by me your days will be multiplied, and years will
be added to your life.

Proverbs 9:11

What a wonderful time is life's autumn
    when the leaves of the trees are all gold,
When God fills each day, as He sends it,
    with memories, priceless and old . . .
What a treasure house filled with rare jewels
    are the blessings of year upon year,
When life has been lived as you've lived it
    in a home where God's presence is dear . . .
And may the deep meaning surrounding this day,
    like the paintbrush of God up above,
Touch your life with wonderful blessings
    and fill your heart brimful with love!

*Artist of artists, You paint such vivid, color-filled, and
ever-changing scenes. Your works are indescribably beautiful. I pray that You send me a sense of appreciation for Your
masterfully created works of art.*

Peace

Perfect Peace

Thou dost keep him in perfect peace, whose mind is stayed on thee, because he trusts in thee. Trust in the Lord for ever, for the Lord God is an everlasting rock.
Isaiah 26:3, 4

God, teach me to be patient—
Teach me to go slow—
Teach me how to "wait on You"
When my way I do not know.
Teach me sweet forbearance
When things do not go right
So I remain unruffled
When others grow uptight.
Teach me how to quiet
My racing, rising heart
So I may hear the answer
You are trying to impart.
Teach me to let go, dear God,
And pray undisturbed until
My heart is filled with inner peace
And I learn to know Your will!

Loving Jesus, You permitted Your will to become God's will. Assist me in letting my will become His will in small and large problems.

For I know the plans I have for you, says the Lord, plans for welfare and not for evil, to give you a future and a hope.

Jeremiah 29:11

> Although it sometimes seems to us
>   our prayers have not been heard,
> God always knows our every need
>   without a single word.
> And He will not forsake us
>   even though the way seems steep,
> For always He is near to us
>   a tender watch to keep.
> And in good times He'll answer us
>   and in His love He'll send
> Greater things than we have asked
>   and blessings without end.
> So though we do not understand
>   why trouble comes to man
> Can we not be contented
>   just to know that it's God's plan.

God, Your plan is a complex one and filled with many questions. If I look and listen there is an answer but it takes effort on my part. Motivate me to seek proper answers.

Blessed be the God and Father of our Lord Jesus Christ! By his great mercy we have been born anew to a living hope through the resurrection of Jesus Christ from the dead, and to an inheritance which is imperishable, undefiled, and unfading, kept in heaven for you, who by God's power are guarded through faith for a salvation ready to be revealed in the last time.

1 Peter 1:3, 4

Death is just another step
along life's changing way,
No more than just a gateway
to a new and better day,
And parting from our loved ones
is much easier to bear
When we know that they are waiting
for us to join them there.
For it is on the wings of death
that the living soul takes flight
Into the Promised Land of God
where there shall be no night.

Today I am feeling a sense of sorrow, a feeling of loss, yet I take real delight and satisfaction in recalling the wonderful memories of the times I shared with my loved one. Jesus, I know the two of you will enjoy good times in eternity together.

Look Up

"Now when these things begin to take place, look up and raise your heads, because your redemption is drawing near."

Luke 21:28

It's easy to grow downhearted
    when nothing goes your way,
It's easy to be discouraged
    when you have a troublesome day,
But trouble is only a challenge
    to spur you on to achieve
The best that God has to offer
    if you have the faith to believe!

Heavenly Father, help me to minimize my problems and maximize my blessings. Develop within me a "What can I do for You?" attitude rather than a "What's in it for me?" outlook. Stop me from being a "fault finder." Make me a "problem solver."

And this world is fading away, and these evil, forbidden things will go with it, but whoever keeps doing the will of God will live forever.

1 John 2:17 TLB

God did not promise sun without rain,
    light without darkness, or joy without pain.
He only promised us strength for the day
    when the darkness comes and we lose our way,
For only through sorrow do we grow more aware
    that God is our refuge in times of despair.
For when we are happy and life's bright and fair,
    we often forget to kneel down in prayer,
But God seems much closer and needed much more
    when trouble and sorrow stand outside our door.
For then we seek shelter in His wondrous love
    and we ask Him to send us help from above.
And that is the reason we know it is true
    that bright, shining hours and dark, sad ones, too,
Are part of the plan God made for each one,
    and all we can pray is, "Thy will be done!"

You really do know what is best for me. Often I cannot see things Your way but don't give up on me, Lord. Stay with me and finish molding me as You see fit.

Besides this you know what hour it is, how it is full time now for you to wake from sleep. For salvation is nearer to us now than when we first believed; the night is far gone, the day is at hand. Let us then cast off the works of darkness and put on the armor of light.

Romans 13:11, 12

Sometimes when a light
goes out of our life
and we are left
in darkness
and do not know which way to go,
we must put our hand
into the hand of God
and ask Him to lead us . . .
and if we let our life
become a prayer
until we are strong enough
to stand under the weight
of our own thoughts again,
somehow even the most difficult
hours are bearable.

My Dear God, let my finest hours be the ones I share with You. If a prayer is a reverent and devout petition, a supplication, or an expression of gratitude offered to you, God, then permit my life to be one long, continuous prayer.

. . . but they who wait for the Lord shall renew their
strength, they shall mount up with wings like eagles,
they shall run and not be weary, they shall walk and
not faint.

Isaiah 40:31

How little we know what God has in store
As daily He blesses our lives more and more.
I've lived many years and learned many things,
But today I have grown "new spiritual wings,"
For pain has a way of broadening our view
And bringing us closer in sympathy, too,
To those who are living in constant pain
And trying somehow to bravely sustain
The faith and endurance to keep on trying
When they'd almost welcome the peace of dying.
And without this experience I would have lived and
    died
Without fathoming the pain of Christ crucified,
For none of us know what pain's all about
Until our "spiritual wings" start to sprout.
So thank You, God, for the "gift" You sent
To teach me that pain is heaven-sent.

*My understanding Lord, permit my love for You to mount
to the heights that only eagles fly. May it continue to soar
with the strength of an eagle.*

The apostles said to the Lord, "Increase our faith!"
And the Lord said, "If you had faith as a grain of
mustard seed, you could say to this sycamine tree,
'Be rooted up, and be planted in the sea,' and it
would obey you."

Luke 17:5, 6

> When the way seems long
>   And the day is dark,
> And we can't hear the song
>   Of the thrush or the lark,
> And our hearts are heavy
>   With worry and care
> And we are lost
>   in the depths of despair.
> That is the time
>   when faith alone
> Can lead us out of
>   the dark unknown,
> For all we really ever need
> Is faith as a grain
>   of mustard seed
> For all God asks
>   is, "Do you believe?"
> And if you do "ye shall receive!"

Permit my faith to take root and to continue to grow.

But as for me, I will look to the LORD,
 I will put my trust in God my savior;
my God will hear me!

Micah 7:7 NAB

Why things happen as they do
We do not always know,
And we cannot always fathom
Why our spirits sink so low.
We flounder in our dark distress,
We are wavering and unstable,
But when we're most inadequate
The Lord God's always able.
And all that is required of us
Whenever things go wrong
Is to trust in God implicitly
With a faith that's deep and strong.
So remember, there's no cloud too dark
For God's light to penetrate
If we keep on believing
And have faith enough to wait!

When I am the weakest, Lord, You are the strongest force on which I can depend. Remind me to call upon You more often than I do. I cannot get myself through the storms, but You can.

In this you rejoice, though now for a little while you may have to suffer various trials, so that the genuineness of your faith, more precious than gold which though perishable is tested by fire, may redound to praise and glory and honor at the revelation of Jesus Christ.

1 Peter 1:6, 7

God, widen my vision so I may see
    the afflictions You have sent to me,
Not as a cross too heavy to wear
    that weights me down in gloomy despair,
Not as something to hate and despise
    but a gift of love sent in disguise,
Something to draw me closer to You
    to teach me patience and forbearance, too,
Something to show me more clearly the way
    to serve You and love You more every day,
Something priceless and precious and rare
    that will keep me forever safe in Thy care
Aware of the spiritual strength that is mine
    when my selfish, small will is lost in Thine!

My life is filled with problems just as everyone's life is. I cannot solve all the problems, but with Your help, Almighty God, I can learn to manage those problems.

Many are the afflictions of the righteous; but the Lord delivers him out of them all.

Psalm 34:19

> If I never grew weary
>   with the weight of my load
> Would I search for God's peace
>   at the end of the road;
> If I never knew sickness
>   and never felt pain
> Would I reach for a hand
>   to help and sustain;
> If I walked not with sorrow
>   and lived without loss
> Would my soul seek sweet solace
>   at the foot of the cross?
> I ask myself this
>   and the answer is plain—
> If my life were all pleasure
>   and I never knew pain
> I'd seek God less often
>   and need Him much less,
> For God's sought more often
>   in time of distress.

My burdens, my heartaches, my sorrows are all lifted and lightened by You, dear God. You listen whenever I complain and I complain often. Would I find time to speak with You if I had no burdens, heartaches, or sorrows? I hope so!

Unfailing Mercy

But thou, O Lord, art a God merciful and gracious, slow to anger and abounding in steadfast love and faithfulness.

Psalm 86:15

What more can we ask of the Savior
Than to know we are never alone,
That His mercy and love are unfailing
And He makes all our problems His own.

Merciful Savior, thank You for walking and talking with me and for sharing my problems. It's important for me to express thanks to You, Lord, because gratitude is best when expressed.

34

There is gold, and abundance of costly stones; but the
lips of knowledge are a precious jewel.

Proverbs 20:15

We watch the rich and famous
Bedecked in precious jewels,
Enjoying earthly pleasures,
Defying moral rules—
And in our mood of discontent
We sink into despair
And long for earthly riches
And feel cheated of our share.
But stop these idle musings,
God has stored up for you
Treasures that are far beyond
Earth's jewels and riches, too—
For never, never discount
What God has promised man
If he will walk in meekness
And accept God's flawless plan.
For if we heed His teachings
As we journey through the years,
We'll find the richest jewels of all
Are crystalized from tears.

*Give me honesty to be myself! Holy Spirit, stay with me.
May I never pretend to be someone or something other than
what and who I am.*

Prayer

God's Presence

For I am sure that neither death, nor life, nor angels, nor principalities, nor things present, nor things to come, nor powers, nor height, nor depth, nor anything else in all creation, will be able to separate us from the love of God in Christ Jesus our Lord.

Romans 8:38, 39

God's love endureth forever—
What a wonderful thing to know
When the tides of life run against you
And your spirit is downcast and low.
God's kindness is ever around you,
Always ready to freely impart
Strength to your faltering spirit,
Cheer to your lonely heart.
God's presence is ever beside you,
As near as the reach of your hand,
You have but to tell Him your troubles,
There is nothing He won't understand.
So wait with a heart that is patient
For the goodness of God to prevail—
For never do prayers go unanswered,
And His mercy and love never fail.

Dear God, I sense Your presence around me, yet I feel so all alone. Help me to overcome these feelings of being deserted.

Brethren, I do not consider that I have made it my own; but one thing I do, forgetting what lies behind and straining forward to what lies ahead, I press on toward the goal for the prize of the upward call of God in Christ Jesus.

Philippians 3:13, 14

If we send no ships out,
 no ships will come in,
And unless there's a contest,
 nobody can win.
For games can't be won
 unless they are played
And prayers can't be answered
 unless they are prayed.
So whatever is wrong
 with your life today,
You'll find a solution
 if you just kneel and pray
But pray for a purpose
 to make life worth living,
And pray for the joy
 of unselfish giving,
For great is your gladness
 and rich your reward
When you make your life's purpose
 the choice of the Lord.

Father, when trials, temptations, and disappointments come my way, let me view them as opportunities to develop endurance as I train for the game of life.

Yet have regard to the prayer of thy servant and to his supplication, O Lord my God, hearkening to the cry and to the prayer which thy servant prays before thee this day; that thy eyes may be open night and day toward this house, the place of which thou has said, "My name shall be there," that thou mayest hearken to the prayer which thy servant offers toward this place.

1 Kings 8:28, 29

Prayers are the stairs
We must climb every day,
If we would reach God
There is no other way,
For we learn to know God
When we meet Him in prayer
And ask Him to lighten
Our burden of care—
So start in the morning
And, though the way's steep,
Climb ever upward
'Til your eyes close in sleep—
For prayers are the stairs
That lead to the Lord,
And to meet Him in prayer
Is the climber's reward.

God, help me to remember that I am special in Your sight, that You care about me, and that You are watching as I climb the stairs to reach You.

For I, the Lord your God, hold your right hand; it is I who say to you, "Fear not, I will help you."

Isaiah 41:13

When we are deeply disturbed with problems
And our minds are filled with doubt
And we struggle to find a solution
But there seems to be no way out,
And finally exhausted and weary,
Discouraged and downcast and low,
With no foreseeable answer
And with no other place to go,
We kneel down in sheer desperation
And slowly and stumblingly pray,
Then impatiently wait for an answer
Which we fully expect right away . . .
And then, when God does not answer,
In one, sudden instant we say,
"God does not seem to be listening,
So why should we bother to pray". . .
But God can't get through to the anxious
Who are much too impatient to wait—
You have to believe in God's promise
That He comes not too soon or too late.

Father, help me to eliminate my anxious prayers by having faith in You. For if I trust in You, I shall not worry and if I worry, I am not trusting in You.

The Key of Prayer

Give ear to my prayer, O God; and hide not thyself
from my supplication! Attend to me, and answer
me. . . .

Psalm 55:1, 2

> Often we pause and wonder
> When we kneel down to pray—
> Can God really hear
> The prayers that we say . . .
> But if we keep praying
> And talking to Him,
> He'll brighten the soul
> That was clouded and dim,
> And as we continue
> Our burden seems lighter,
> Our sorrow is softened
> And our outlook is brighter—
> For though we feel helpless
> And alone when we start
> Our prayer is the key
> That opens the heart.

*Dear Lord, Your hands are gentle yet strong. Help me to
place my life in Your hands every day.*

It is he who made the earth by his power, who established the world by his wisdom, and by his understanding stretched out the heavens.

Jeremiah 10:12

No problem is too intricate
And no sorrow that we face
Is too deep and devastating
To be softened by His grace,
No trials and tribulations
Are beyond what we can bear
If we share them with our Father
As we talk to Him in prayer—
God asks for no credentials,
He accepts us with our flaws,
He is kind and understanding
And He welcomes us because
We are His erring children
And He loves us every one,
And He freely and completely
Forgives all we have done,
Asking only if we're ready
To follow where He leads—
Content that in His wisdom
He will answer all our needs.

Dear God, I am reaching for You. With all sincerity I want to follow You.

Blessed is the man who endures trial, for when he has stood the test he will receive the crown of life which God has promised to those who love him.

James 1:12

The stairway rises heaven-high—
The steps are dark and steep,
In weariness we climb them
As we stumble, fall, and weep.
And many times we falter
Along the path of prayer
Wondering if You hear us
And if You really care . . .
Oh, give us some assurance,
Restore our faith anew,
So we can keep on climbing
The stairs of prayer to You—
For we are weak and wavering,
Uncertain and unsure,
And only meeting You in prayer
Can help us to endure
All life's trials and troubles,
Its sickness, pain, and sorrow,
And give us strength and courage
To face and meet tomorrow!

With each step I climb closer to You, Lord. Help me to remember that if I concentrate on the regrets and sorrows of yesterday and dwell on the worries of tomorrow, I have no energy left to be thankful for today.

. . . every one who keeps the sabbath, and does not profane it, and holds fast my covenant—these I will bring to my holy mountain, and make them joyful in my house of prayer; their burnt offerings and their sacrifices will be accepted on my altar; for my house shall be called a house of prayer for all peoples.

Isaiah 56:6–8

Just close your eyes
and open your heart
And feel your worries
and cares depart,
Just yield yourself
to the Father above
And let Him hold you
secure in His love.
So when you are tired,
discouraged, and blue,
There's always one door
that is open to you—
That is the door
to the house of prayer
And you'll find God waiting
to meet you there.

Enter often into the house of prayer. Wherever its location is for you, be assured that God will be waiting for you.

"And now about prayer. When you pray, don't be like the hypocrites who pretend piety by praying publicly on street corners and in the synagogues where everyone can see them. Truly, that is all the reward they will ever get. But when you pray, go away by yourself, all alone, and shut the door behind you and pray to your Father secretly, and your Father, who knows your secrets, will reward you."

Matthew 6:5–8 TLB

Is it measured words that are memorized,
Forcefully said and dramatized,
Offered with pomp and with arrogant pride
In words unmatched to the feelings inside?
No . . . prayer is so often just words unspoken,
Whispered in tears by a heart that is broken.
For God is already deeply aware
Of the burdens we find too heavy to bear,
And all we need do is to seek Him in prayer
And without a word He will help us to bear
Our trials and troubles—our sickness and sorrow
And show us the way to a brighter tomorrow.
There's no need at all for impressive prayer
For the minute we seek God He is already there!

I want to talk with You, God, but so do so many others. How can You listen to all of us at one time? Somehow, You find a way. As I wait for Your answer, I feel my burdens lifted. Thank You for listening.

Therefore, since we are justified by faith, we have peace with God through our Lord Jesus Christ. Through him we have obtained access to this grace in which we stand, and we rejoice in our hope of sharing the glory of God.

Romans 5:1, 2

> I'm way down here!
>   You're way up there!
> Are You sure You can hear
>   My faint, faltering prayer?
> For I'm so unsure
>   Of just how to pray—
> To tell you the truth, God,
>   I don't know what to say . . .
> I just know I am lonely
>   And vaguely disturbed,
> Bewildered and restless,
>   Confused and perturbed . . .
> And they tell me that prayer
>   Helps to quiet the mind
> And unburden the heart
>   For in stillness we find
> A newborn assurance
>   That Someone does care
> And Someone does answer
>   Each small sincere prayer!

Do You hear me, God? Do You really listen when I pray? . . . Yes, I believe You do. I can sense Your presence even now.

Be merciful to me, O God, be merciful to me, for in
thee my soul takes refuge; in the shadow of thy wings
I will take refuge; till the storms of destruction pass
by.

Psalm 57:1

When the storms of life
        gather darkly ahead,
I think of these wonderful words
        I once read
And I say to myself
        as threatening clouds hover,
"Don't fold up your wings
        and run for cover
But like the eagle
        spread wide your wings
And soar far above
        the troubles life brings."
For the eagle knows
        that the higher he flies
The more tranquil and brighter
        become the skies.
And there is nothing in life
        God ever asks us to bear
That we can't soar above
        on the wings of prayer.

*Dear God, give my prayers the power of an eagle's wings.
Give me the tenacity of an eagle and the courage to ride out
the storms of life, to soar above the threatening clouds and
to locate the shelter that You alone provide.*

Commitment

"And how does a man benefit if he gains the whole world and loses his soul in the process? For is anything worth more than his soul!"

Mark 8:36, 37 TLB

In this world of new concepts
    it has often been said—
Why heed the Commandments
    of a God who is dead,
And yet this "dead God"
    still holds in His hand
The star-studded sky,
    the sea, and the land,
And with perfect precision
    the old earth keeps spinning
As flawlessly accurate
    as in the beginning.
So be not deceived
    by the new pharisees
Who boast man has only
    his own self to please,
And what, though man gain
    the whole world and its pleasures,
If he loses his soul
    and eternity's treasures?

Father, help me to keep my priorities in proper order. Assist me in keeping Your Commandments and let me love You with my whole heart and let me love my neighbor as myself. God, You are very much alive in the world today.

When the perishable puts on the imperishable, and the mortal puts on immortality, then shall come to pass the saying that is written: "Death is swallowed up in victory. O death, where is thy victory? O death, where is thy sting?" The sting of death is sin, and the power of sin is the law. But thanks be to God, who gives us the victory through our Lord Jesus Christ.

1 Corinthians 15:54–57

In this restless world of struggle
It is very hard to find
Answers to the questions
That daily come to mind—
We cannot see the future,
What's beyond is still unknown,
For the secret of God's Kingdom
Still belongs to Him alone—
But He granted us salvation
When His Son was crucified,
For life became immortal
Because our Savior died.

Glory and praise to You, Lord Jesus! You granted life eternal to me when You were crucified. I pray that I appreciate properly Your great sacrifice. Because You live, I live also.

On the third day there was a marriage at Cana in Galilee, and the mother of Jesus was there; Jesus also was invited to the marriage, with his disciples. When the wine gave out, the mother of Jesus said to him, "They have no wine." And Jesus said to her, "O woman, what have you to do with me? My hour has not yet come." His mother said to the servants, "Do whatever he tells you."

John 2:1–5

Your hearts are filled with happiness
    so great and overflowing.
You cannot comprehend it
    for it's far beyond all knowing
You wish that you could capture it
    and never let it go
So you might walk forever
    in its radiant magic glow . . .
But love in all its ecstasy
    is such a fragile thing,
Like gossamer in cloudless skies
    or a hummingbird's small wing,
But love that lasts forever
    must be made of something strong,
The kind of strength that's gathered
    when the heart can hear no song.

Marrying does not a marriage make. It takes loving, caring, forgiving, sacrificing, and always the sharing of the home with You, God, as the unseen but welcome Guest at each meal and as the silent Listener to every conversation.

The Lord redeems the life of his servants; none of those who take refuge in him will be condemned.

Psalm 34:22

In a myriad of miraculous ways
God shapes our lives and changes our days,
Beyond our will or even knowing
God keeps our spirit ever growing.
For lights and shadows, sun and rain,
Sadness and gladness, joy and pain,
Combine to make our lives complete
And give us victory through defeat . . .
"Oh, Love Divine, All Love Excelling,"
In troubled hearts You just keep dwelling,
Patiently waiting for a "Prodigal Son"
To say at last, "Thy will be done."

Lord, shape me, change me, keep my spirit growing through the sharing of Your love divine, all love excelling.

Let not sin therefore reign in your mortal bodies, to make you obey their passions. Do not yield your members to sin as instruments of wickedness, but yield yourselves to God as men who have been brought from death to life, and your members to God as instruments of righteousness.

Romans 6:12, 13

> Sin is much more
>   than an act or a deed,
> More than "false witness"
>   or avarice and greed,
> More than adultery
>   or killing and stealing,
> Sin starts with a thought
>   or an unworthy feeling.
> It's something we nurture and then cultivate
> By conjuring up evils,
>   we then imitate,
> And the longer we dwell
>   on this evil within
> The greater our urge
>   and desire to sin,
> So ask God to help you
>   to conquer desire
> Aroused by the thoughts
>   that have set you afire.

My Christian maturity needs refinishing and polishing. Prince of Peace, please help me to accomplish this chore and transform me into an instrument of righteousness.

Again Jesus spoke to them, saying, "I am the light of the world; he who follows me will not walk in darkness, but will have the light of life."

John 8:12

I am the way
    so just follow Me
Though the way be rough
    and you cannot see.
I am the truth
    which all men seek
So heed not false prophets
    nor the words that they speak . . .
I am the life
    and I hold the key
That opens the door
    to eternity . . .
And in this dark world
    I am the light
To the Promised Land
    where there is no night!

Jesus, You are the light of the world. Let a little of Your radiance shine on me so that I can be a beacon of light to a weary and lost traveler on this road of life.

"You are my witnesses," says the Lord, "and my servant whom I have chosen, that you may know and believe me and understand that I am He."

Isaiah 43:10

When we are confirmed
    in the faith of the Lord,
Our greatest possession
    and richest reward
Is knowing that now
    we are heralds of the King,
Ready His praises and glory to sing.
Confirmed in the faith
    and upheld by His hand,
Eager to follow His smallest command.
Secure in the knowledge
    that though now and then
We're guilty of sins
    that are common to men,
He freely forgives
    and understands, too,
And there's nothing—no, nothing
    that God cannot do.

Confirm my faith in You, Lord, and let me dedicate my life to You and to the following of Your Commandments.

The point is this: he who sows sparingly will also reap sparingly, and he who sows bountifully will also reap bountifully. Each one must do as he has made up his mind, not reluctantly or under compulsion, for God loves a cheerful giver. And God is able to provide you with every blessing in abundance, so that you may always have enough of everything and may provide in abundance for every good work.

2 Corinthians 9:6–8

The more you give,
    the more you get—
The more you laugh,
    the less you fret—
The more of everything
    you share,
The more you'll always
    have to spare—
The more you love,
    the more you'll find
That life is good
    and friends are kind.
For only what
    we give away,
Enriches us
    from day to day.

Compassionate Father, help me put aside my selfish thoughts and be more like You. I need You, God, every day.

The Lord is not slow about his promise as some count slowness, but is forbearing toward you, not wishing that any should perish, but that all should reach repentance.

2 Peter 3:9

He sent His Son to live on earth
And to walk with sinful men,
And the problems that confront us
Are the same today as then,
For vice and crime and evil
Prevailed in Rome and Greece
And power-driven demagogues
Incited war, not peace—
Depraved, debauched, and dissolute,
Men lusted after pleasure,
They knew no god but power
And gold was their only treasure.
So let no one mislead you
With that hackneyed little phrase
That there's a "many-century gap"
Between God and modern days
For God knows that we are headed for
The same, grim, terrible fate
Unless man is awakened
Before the hour's too late.

Jesus, in the past You died for us. In these present times You live for us and You encourage us. In the future You will call for us. You are a Savior for all times.

Keep the Faith

I have fought the good fight, I have finished the race,
I have kept the faith.

2 Timothy 4:7

> Cling to your standards
>   and fight the good fight,
> Take a firm stand
>   for things that are right,
> And let nothing sway you
>   or turn you away.
> From God's old Commandments—
>   they are still new today.

*Loving Savior, when temptations come my way be with me
as I reflect upon how You handled Your temptations. With
sincere interest and purpose of mind, encourage me to ask,
"What would Jesus do in this situation?"*

"Truly I say to you, unless you turn and become like children, you will never enter the kingdom of heaven. Whoever humbles himself like this child, he is the greatest in the kingdom of heaven."

Matthew 18:3, 4

Hear me, Blessed Jesus
    as I say my prayers today
And tell me You are close to me,
    and You'll never go away,
And tell me that You love me
    like the Bible says You do,
And tell me also, Jesus,
    I can always come to You
And You will understand me
    when other people don't,
And though some may forget me
    just tell me that You won't—
And, Jesus, stay real close to me
    at home and school and play,
For I will feel much braver
    if You're never far away—
And someday when I'm older
    I will show You it is true
That even as a little child
    My heart belonged to You.

Tender and gentle Shepherd, hold me in Your arms, carry me when I have lost my way. Guide me to the path that leads to You.

But you, beloved, build yourselves up on your most holy faith; pray in the Holy Spirit; keep yourselves in the love of God; wait for the mercy of our Lord Jesus Christ unto eternal life.

Jude 20, 21

Everything in life is passing
    and whatever we possess
Cannot endure forever
    but ends in nothingness,
So all that man acquires,
    be it power, fame, or jewels,
Is but limited and earthly,
    only "treasure made for fools."
For only in God's Kingdom
    can man find enduring treasure,
Priceless gifts of love and beauty
    more than mortal man can measure,
And the riches he accumulates
    he can keep and part with never,
For only in God's Kingdom
    do our treasures last forever . . .
So use the word *forever*
    with sanctity and love,
For nothing is forever
    but the love of God above.

Dear God, may I always recognize the true value of the greatest gift in this world or the next—Your eternal love for me.

But Jesus looked at them and said to them, "With men this is impossible, but with God all things are possible."

Matthew 19:26

Nothing is ever too hard to do
If your faith is strong and your purpose is true . . .
So never give up and never stop
Just journey on to the mountaintop!

Holy Spirit, be with me when I walk the valleys and the mountains of my life. Let me rejoice over heights climbed and depths conquered.

Friendship

For what will it profit a man, if he gains the whole world and forfeits his life?

Matthew 16:26

> Amid stresses and strains
>   much too many to mention,
> And pressure-packed days
>   filled with turmoil and tension,
> We seldom have time
>   to be friendly or kind
> For we're harassed and hurried
>   and always behind—
> And while we've more gadgets
>   and buttons to press
> Making leisure hours greater
>   and laboring hours less.
> What does it matter
>   if man reaches his goal
> And gains the whole world
>   but loses his soul—
> For what have we won,
>   if in gaining this end
> We've been much too busy
>   to be kind to a friend?

What can I do today to show kindness to friend? Make a telephone call to someone who is lonely? Send a note to someone who is ill? Visit an elderly person? Direct my path, Lord. Where You lead, I shall try to follow.

Extend a Hand

In all things I have shown you that by so toiling one must help the weak, remembering the words of the Lord Jesus, how he said, "It is more blessed to give than to receive."

Acts 20:35

In this troubled world
    it's refreshing to find
Someone who still has
    the time to be kind,
Someone who still has
    the faith to believe
That the more you give
    the more you receive,
Someone who's ready
    by thought, word, or deed
To reach out a hand
    in the hour of need.

Father, place within me the ability and the desire to extend my hand willingly and frequently to others. Encourage me to stop and visit with the lonely, to sit and listen to the discouraged, to offer a smile to the sad, and to create a little more warmth in this cold world, wherever I may be.

Then they also will answer, "Lord, when did we see thee hungry or thirsty or a stranger or naked or sick or in prison, and did not minister to thee?" Then he will answer them, "Truly, I say to you, as you did it not to one of the least of these, you did it not to me."

Matthew 25:44, 45

On life's busy thoroughfares
We meet with angels unawares—
But we are too busy to listen or hear,
Too busy to sense that God is near,
Too busy to stop and recognize
The grief that lies in another's eyes,
Too busy to offer to help or share,
Too busy to sympathize or care,
Too busy to do the good things we should,
Telling ourselves we would if we could . . .
But life is too swift and the pace is too great
And we dare not pause for we might be late.
And we tell ourselves there will come a day
We will have more time to pause on our way . . .
But before we know it "life's sun has set"
And we've passed the Savior but never met,
For hurrying along life's thoroughfare
We passed Him by and remained unaware
That within the very sight of our eye,
Unnoticed, the Son of God passed by.

My living and loving Savior, please help me to really know people and to recognize You in them.

But I, O Lord, cry to thee; in the morning my prayer comes before thee.

Psalm 88:13

Often during a busy day
I pause for a minute
    to silently pray,
I mention the names
    of those I love
And treasured friends
    I am fondest of—
For it doesn't matter
    where we pray
If we honestly mean
    the words that we say,
For God is always
    listening to hear
The prayers that are
    made by a heart that's sincere.

Loving God, bless all my friends today and bless those who are not yet my friends, in other words, God, bless us one and all.

A friend loves at all times. . . .

Proverbs 17:17

Among the great and glorious gifts
    our Heavenly Father sends
Is the gift of understanding
    that we find in loving friends,
For in this world of trouble
    that is filled with anxious care
Everybody needs a friend
    in whom they're free to share.
So when we need some sympathy
    or a friendly hand to touch,
Or an ear that listens tenderly
    and speaks words that mean so much,
We seek our true and trusted friend
    in the knowledge that we'll find
A heart that's sympathetic
    and an understanding mind.

Father, develop within me the qualities necessary for being "a good and true friend." Teach me to be considerate and to take time to be a good listener when attentive listening is needed.

Beloved, let us love one another; for love is of God, and he who loves is born of God and knows God. He who does not love does not know God; for God is love.

1 John 4:7, 8

A warm, ready smile
    or a kind, thoughtful deed,
Or a hand outstretched
    in an hour of need
Can change our whole outlook
    and make the world bright
Where a minute before
    just nothing seemed right—
It's a wonderful world,
    and it always will be
If we keep our eyes open
    and focused to see
The wonderful things
    we are capable of
When we open our hearts
    to God and His love.

God of love, love me always. Enable me to put into practice the act of doing a kindly deed every day, no matter how small that good deed may be. Accomplishing a small deed has more meaning than the largest good intention left undone.

The Gift of Friendship

Two are better than one, because they have a good
reward for their toil. For if they fall, one will lift up his
fellow; but woe to him who is alone when he falls and
has not another to lift him up.

Ecclesiastes 4:9, 10

Friendship is a priceless gift
that cannot be bought or sold,
But its value is far greater
than a mountain made of gold—
For gold is cold and lifeless,
it can neither see nor hear,
And in the time of trouble
it is powerless to cheer—
It has no ears to listen,
no heart to understand,
It cannot bring you comfort
or reach out a helping hand—
So when you ask God for a gift,
be thankful if He sends
Not diamonds, pearls, or riches,
but the love of real true friends.

*Thank You God, for sending me the treasure of a true
friend. My friend stays at my side when all others leave me.
My friend is like You in that regard.*

And as you wish that men would do to you, do so to
them.

Luke 6:31

Friendship is a golden chain,
The links are friends so dear,
And like a rare and precious jewel
It's treasured more each year . . .
It's clasped together firmly
With a love that's deep and true,
And it's rich with happy memories
And fond recollections, too . . .
Time can't destroy its beauty
For, as long as memory lives,
Years can't erase the pleasure
That the joy of friendship gives . . .
For friendship is a priceless gift
That can't be bought or sold,
But to have an understanding friend
Is worth far more than gold . . .
And the golden chain of friendship
Is a strong and blessed tie
Binding kindred hearts together
As the years go passing by.

*Thank You, God, for sending friendship into the world.
True friendship finds its foundation in the parable of the
Good Samaritan, the Sermon on the Mount, and the Golden
Rule.*

Wings of Love

How precious is thy steadfast love, O God! The children of men take refuge in the shadow of thy wings. They feast on the abundance of thy house, and thou givest them drink from the river of thy delights.

Psalm 36:7, 8

The priceless gift of life is love
For with the help of God above
Love can change the human race
And make this world a better place.
For love dissolves all hate and fear
And makes our vision bright and clear
So we can see and rise above
Our pettiness on wings of love.

Father, keep me levelheaded, even when righteous indignation is justified. Let me be understanding and kind and forgiving.

Faith

Then Jesus told him, "You believe because you have
seen me. But blessed are those who haven't seen me
and believe anyway."

John 20:29 TLB

"I have no faith," the skeptic cries,
"I can only accept what I see with my eyes."
Yet man has to have faith or he would never
        complete
Just a simple task like crossing the street,
For he has to have faith in his manly stride
To get him across to the other side,
And the world would be panic-stricken indeed
If no one thought that he could succeed
In doing the smallest, simplest thing
That life with its many demands can bring . . .
So why do the skeptics still ridicule
And call "the man of faith" a fool
When faith is the basis of all that we do—
And that includes unbelievers, too.

*Holy Spirit, whether I cross the street or cross from life to
death, keep my faith alive and stay with me.*

And they were bringing children to him, that he might touch them; and the disciples rebuked them. But when Jesus saw it he was indignant, and said to them, "Let the children come to me, do not hinder them; for to such belongs the kingdom of God. Truly, I say to you, whoever does not receive the kingdom of God like a child shall not enter it." And he took them in his arms and blessed them, laying his hands upon them.

Mark 10:13–16

"Jesus loves me, this I know,
　　For the Bible tells me so"—
　　Little children ask no more,
　　　　For love is all they're looking for,
And in a small child's shining eyes
The faith of all the ages lies—
For faith in things we cannot see
Requires a child's simplicity.
And, with a small child's trusting eyes,
May all men come to realize
That faith alone can save man's soul
　　and lead him to a higher goal.

Master, You taught that fancy words, a big vocabulary, power, and wealth are not necessary to reach the highest goal. What is needed is a true, sincere, and childlike faith. Grant that kind of faith to me.

The works of his hands are faithful and just; all his precepts are trustworthy, they are established for ever and ever, to be performed with faithfulness and uprightness.

Psalm 111:7, 8

There is really nothing we need know
or even try to understand
If we refuse to be discouraged
and trust God's guiding hand . . .
So take heart and meet each minute
with faith in God's great love,
Aware that every day of life
is controlled by God above . . .
And never dread tomorrow
or what the future brings,
Just pray for strength and courage
and trust God in all things . . .
And never grow discouraged
be patient and just wait
For God never comes too early
and He never comes too late!

Infuse me, God, with optimism and trust. I shall put forth my best effort and then leave the rest to You.

God's Magnificent Light

But know that the Lord has set apart the godly for himself; the Lord hears when I call to him.

Psalm 4:3

In sickness or health
In suffering or pain,
In storm laden skies,
In sunshine and rain
God always is there
To lighten your way
And lead you through darkness
To a much brighter day.

Father God, one small candle can change the visibility in a darkened room. One little star can light up the sky. Your magnificent light shines forth, enabling a world to see. Place a small glow within me.

76

Have no anxiety about anything, but in everything by prayer and supplication with thanksgiving let your requests be made known to God.

Philippians 4:6, 7

Don't start your day by supposin'
    that trouble is just ahead,
It's better to stop supposin'
    and start with a prayer instead.
And make it a prayer of Thanksgiving
    for the wonderful things God has wrought
Like the beautiful sunrise and sunset,
    God's gifts that are free and not bought—
For what is the use of supposin'
    the dire things that could happen to you
And worrying about some misfortune
    that seldom if ever comes true—
For supposin' the worst things will happen
    only helps to make them come true
And you darken the bright, happy moments
    that the dear Lord has given to you—
So if you desire to be happy
    and get rid of the misery of dread
Just give up supposin' the worst things
    and look for the best things instead.

Today is a new day and I shall meet it with a renewed zest for living and heartfelt thanksgiving to You, God, for Your bountiful gifts.

For with thee is the fountain of life; in thy light do we see light. O continue thy steadfast love to those who know thee, and thy salvation to the upright of heart!

Psalm 36:9, 10

When dark days come,
    and they come to us all,
We feel so helpless
    and lost and small
And when the darkness
    shuts out the light
We must lean on faith
    to restore our sight
For there is nothing
    that we need to know
If we have faith
    that wherever we go
God will be there
    to help us bear
Our disappointments,
    pain and care.

Loving Shepherd, please hold this lamb in Your arms with tender security and keep me close to Your heart.

"Behold, God is my salvation; I will trust, and will not be afraid; for the Lord God is my strength and my song, and he has become my salvation." With joy you will draw water from the wells of salvation. And you will say in that day: "Give thanks to the Lord, call upon his name; make known his deeds among the nations, proclaim that his name is exalted. Sing praises to the Lord, for he has done gloriously; let this be known in all the earth."

Isaiah 12:2–5

Oh, Blessed Father, hear this prayer
   and keep all of us in Your care.
You are so great . . .
   we are so small . . .
And when trouble comes
   as it does to us all
There's so little that we can do
   except to place our trust in You!
So place yourself in His loving care
   And He will gladly help you bear
Whatever lies ahead of you
   and God will see you safely through
For no earthly pain is ever too much
   if God bestows His merciful touch.

Problems that come my way are not mine to choose, Father, but the manner in which I react to those problems is my decision. Help me respond in the right way.

Give Me Strength

The Lord will fulfil his purpose for me; thy steadfast love, O Lord, endures for ever. Do not forsake the work of thy hands.

Psalm 138:8

Bless me, Heavenly Father, forgive my erring ways,
Grant me strength to serve Thee, put purpose in my
    days.
Give me understanding, enough to make me kind
So I may judge all people with my heart and not my
    mind.
And teach me to be patient in everything I do,
Content to trust Your wisdom and follow after You
And help me when I falter and hear me when I pray
And receive me in Your Kingdom to dwell with You
    someday.

Father, help me to know the purpose that You have in mind for me alone to fulfill and then give me strength to accomplish it.

Our soul waits for the Lord; he is our help and shield.
Yea, our heart is glad in him, because we trust in his
holy name.

Psalm 33:20, 21

> For there are certain periods when the soul
>   is sweetly sad
> As it contemplates the mystery
>   of both good times and bad.
> We're not really discontented
>   and we are never unaware
> That the good Lord up in heaven
>   has us always in His care,
> But the soul of man is restless
>   and it just keeps longing for
> A haven that is safe and sure
>   that will last forevermore . . .
> And as I sit here writing this
>   a thought passed through my mind—
> "Why dwell on past or future
>   or what's ahead or gone behind?
> Just follow God unquestioningly
>   because you love him so,
> For if you trust His judgment
>   there is nothing you need know!"

*Keep my faith strong, God, even though I cannot always see
a visible sign of You at work, I do believe You are working
and watching every minute of every day.*

The steps of a man are from the Lord, and he establishes him in whose way he delights.

Psalm 37:23

Into our lives come many things
    to break the dull routine,
The things we had not planned on
    that happen unforeseen,
The unexpected little joys
    that are scattered on our way,
Success we did not count on
    or a rare, fulfilling day.
The unplanned sudden meeting
    that comes with sweet surprise
And lights the heart with happiness
    like a rainbow in the skies . . .
Now some folks call it fickle fate
And some folks call it chance,
While others just accept it
As a pleasant happenstance—
But no matter what you call it,
It didn't come without design,
For all our lives are fashioned
By the hand that is divine.

Dear God, help me to use properly the gifts that You have given me. May I always remember that it is not the person with the greatest talent who succeeds but rather the individual who keeps the faith and extends his or her talent to its greatest capacity.

His divine power has granted to us all things that pertain to life and godliness, through the knowledge of him who called us to his own glory and excellence, by which he has granted to us his precious and very great promises. . . .

2 Peter 1:3, 4

When you're troubled and worried
    and sick at heart
And your plans are upset,
    and your world falls apart,
Remember God's ready
    and waiting to share
The burden you find
    much too heavy to bear—
So with faith, let go
    and let God lead the way
Into a brighter
    and less-troubled day—
For God has a plan
    for everyone
If we learn to pray,
    "Thy will be done."

Let go and let God! If only I can remember to put this into practice. Inspire me to be a better person and not a bitter one.

We Win by Faith

What is faith? It is the confident assurance that something we want is going to happen. It is the certainty that what we hope for is waiting for us, even though we cannot see it up ahead.

Hebrews 11:1 TLB

Oh, Father, grant once more to men
A simple, childlike faith again,
Forgetting color, race and creed
And seeing only the heart's deep need . . .
For faith alone can save man's soul
And lead him to a higher goal,
For there's but one unfailing course—
We win by faith and not by force.

Father, teach me to trust You and to increase my faith. Eliminate discrimination from my way of life. Keep me from judging others.

The Lord is good, a stronghold in the day of trouble;
he knows those who take refuge in him.

Nahum 1:7

Our Father, up in heaven,
    hear this fervent prayer—
May the people of all nations
    be united in Thy care,
For earth's peace and man's salvation
    can come only by Thy grace
And not through bombs and missiles
    and our quest for outer space . . .
We have come to trust completely
    in the power of man-made things,
Unmindful of God's mighty power
    and that He is "King of Kings" . . .
We have turned our eyes away from Him
    to go our selfish way,
And money, power, and pleasure,
    are the gods we serve today.
Oh, Father, up in heaven,
    stir and wake our sleeping souls,
Renew our faith and lift us up
    and give us higher goals.

*King of Kings, help our nation to see that what each citizen
must do is place his trust in God, as did our forefathers.*

Thankfulness

For from him and through him and to him are all things. To him be glory for ever.

Romans 11:36

Thank You, God, for everything—
    the big things and the small,
For "every good gift comes from God"—
    the giver of them all.
And all too often we accept
    without any thanks or praise
The gifts God sends as blessings
    each day in many ways.
And thank You for the "miracles"
    we are much too blind to see,
Lord, give us new awareness
    of our many gifts from Thee,
And help us to remember
    that the key to life and living
Is to make each prayer a prayer of thanks
    and every day thanksgiving.

Every good gift comes from You, Father, and I am cognizant of that fact. Grant that I never forget it and that I offer to You appropriate gratitude for the abundance of Your gifts, seen and unseen.

For he will deliver you from the snare of the fowler and from the deadly pestilence; he will cover you with his pinions, and under his wings you will find refuge; his faithfulness is a shield and buckler. You will not fear the terror of the night, nor the arrow that flies by day, nor the pestilence that stalks in darkness, nor the destruction that wastes at noonday.

Psalm 91:3–6

More than hearts can imagine
or minds comprehend,
God's bountiful gifts
are ours without end.
We reach for a sunbeam
but the sun still abides,
We draw one short breath
but there's air on all sides.
Whatever we ask for
falls short of God's giving
For His greatness exceeds
every facet of living.
For God has a "storehouse"
just filled to the brim
With all that man needs
if we'll only ask Him.

My cup runneth over and yet You continue to send more blessings my way. Thank You for Your generosity, God.

Be Glad

You will seek me and find me; when you seek me
with all your heart.

Jeremiah 29:13

> Be glad
>   that you've walked
>   in sunshine and rain,
> Be glad
>   that you've felt
>   both pleasure and pain,
> Be glad
>   for the comfort
>   you've found in prayer,
> Be glad
>   for God's blessings . . .
>   His love and His care.

*Father, keep me ever grateful for the trials and the joys that
You send my way. I need the rain to appreciate fully the
sunshine in my life.*

Ascribe to the Lord, O heavenly beings, ascribe to the Lord glory and strength. Ascribe to the Lord the glory of his name; worship the Lord in holy array. The voice of the Lord is upon the waters; the God of glory thunders, the Lord, upon many waters. The voice of the Lord is powerful, the voice of the Lord is full of majesty.

Psalm 29:1–4

You ask me how I know it's true
     That there is a living God—
A God who rules the universe,
     The sky . . . the sea . . . the sod;
A God who holds all creatures
     In the hollow of His hand;
A God who put infinity
     In one tiny grain of sand;
A God who hangs the sun out
     Slowly with the break of day,
And gently takes the stars in
     And puts the night away;
What better answers are there
     To prove His Holy Being
Than the wonders all around us
     That are ours just for the seeing.

Creator of the universe, I marvel at Your power and glory. The wonders of Your mighty handiwork are beyond description. Thank You for sharing Your work with me.

Sun and moon, bless the Lord;
     praise and exalt him above all forever.
Stars of heaven, bless the Lord;
     praise and exalt him above all forever.
Every shower and dew, bless the Lord;
     praise and exalt him above all forever.

Daniel 3:62–64 NAB

Thank You, God, for the beauty
     around me everywhere,
The gentle rain and glistening dew,
     the sunshine and the air,
The joyous gift of feeling
     the soul's soft, whispering voice
That speaks to me from deep within
     and makes my heart rejoice.

My loving Creator, nature is the living but silent language that You have given to us creatures here on earth. The early purple crocus breaking through the late white blanket of snow and all other examples of Your handiwork in nature, declare silently but positively, "God is here."

For the Lord your God is bringing you into a good land, a land of brooks of water, of fountains and springs, flowing forth in valleys and hills, a land of wheat and barley . . . a land in which you will eat bread without scarcity, in which you will lack nothing. . . . And you shall eat and be full, and you shall bless the Lord your God for the good land he has given you.

Deuteronomy 8:7–10

Thanksgiving is more
    than a day in November
That students of history
    are taught to remember,
For while we still offer
    the traditional prayer,
We pray out of habit without being aware
That the Pilgrims thanked God
    just for being alive,
For the strength that He gave them
    to endure and survive.
Oh, teach us, dear God,
    we are all Pilgrims still,
Subject alone to Your guidance and will,
And show us the way
    to purposeful living
So we may have reason
    for daily thanksgiving.

Father, deepen my appreciation of our country and its gifts and let me never forget the source of those gifts and the origin of our spiritual faith.

Remind them to be submissive to rulers and authorities, to be obedient, to be ready for any honest work, to speak evil of no one, to avoid quarreling, to be gentle, and to show perfect courtesy toward all men.

Titus 3:1, 2

Thank You, God,
for little things
that often come our way,
The things we take for granted
but don't mention when we pray—
the unexpected courtesy,
the thoughtful, kindly deed,
A hand reached out to help us
in the time of sudden need—
Oh, make us more aware, dear God,
of little daily graces
That come to us
with sweet surprise
from never-dreamed-of places.

Comforter of all, develop courtesy within me. Forgive me for the times I failed to act when an opportunity to help someone presented itself. Inspire me to recognize these opportunities to be of assistance.

For everything created by God is good, and nothing is to be rejected if it is received with thanksgiving; for then it is consecrated by the word of God and prayer.

1 Timothy 4:4, 5

Take nothing for granted
    for whenever you do
The "joy of enjoying"
    is lessened for you
For we rob our own lives
    much more than we know
When we fail to respond
    or in any way show
Our thanks for the blessings
    that daily are ours,
The warmth of the sun,
    the fragrance of flowers,
The beauty of twilight,
    the freshness of dawn,
The coolness of dew
    on a green velvet lawn,
For the joy of enjoying
    and the fullness of living
Are found in the heart that is
    filled with thanksgiving.

Thank You, God, for the many blessings that You have bestowed upon me. Sometimes I forget to say it, but I am grateful and I do love You.

It is good to give thanks to the Lord, to sing praises to thy name, O Most High; to declare thy steadfast love in the morning, and thy faithfulness by night.

Psalm 92:1, 2

Thank You, God, for little things
    that come unexpectedly
To brighten up a dreary day
    that dawned so dismally.
Thank You, God, for sending
    a happy thought my way
To blot out my depression
    on a disappointing day.
Oh, God, the list is endless
    of things to thank You for,
But I take them all for granted
    and unconsciously ignore
That everything I think or do,
    each movement that I make,
Each measured rhythmic heartbeat,
    each breath of life I take
Is something You have given me
    for which there is no way
For me in all my "smallness"
    to in any way repay.

Please God, let the manner in which I conduct my life be pleasing to You and a thank You in return for all the blessings You have bestowed upon me and my loved ones.

If you found any beauty in the poems of this book
Or some peace and comfort in a word or line
Don't give me praise or wordly acclaim
For the words that you read are not mine . . .
I borrowed them all to share with you
From our Heavenly Father above,
And the joy that you felt was God speaking to you
As He flooded your heart with His Love.

H.S.R.

And if you receive hope or strength
From the Scripture or from the prayer
Know that whenever or wherever you read this,
Our Heavenly Father is there!

V.J.R.